AI Master Guide

The Complete Student Handbook on Applications & Innovation

Amaara Verma & Abeer Verma

Fusion Books

Publisher	**:**	**Fusion Books** X-30, Okhla Industrial Area, Phase-II New Delhi-110020
Phone	:	011- 40712200
E-mail	:	wecare@diamondbooks.in
Website	:	www.diamondbooks.in
Edition	:	2026

Author's Note

Artificial Intelligence is no longer an emerging concept — it is becoming the foundation of modern systems. From healthcare and finance to agriculture, education, governance, and space research, AI is transforming how the world functions.

As students growing up in this era, we realized something important:
Understanding AI is no longer optional.
It is essential.

But understanding AI does not simply mean knowing definitions. It means recognizing how it is applied, how it drives innovation, and how it must be used responsibly.
In this Master Guide, we move beyond basic introductions.
Abeer explores how AI systems are structured — from data pipelines and machine learning models to automation and intelligent applications.

Amaara examines the broader landscape — how AI shapes industries, innovation ecosystems, public policy, ethics, and the future of work.
Together, we present this handbook as a comprehensive yet accessible guide for students who want clarity, not confusion.
This book is not about fear or hype.

It is about informed intelligence.
Because the future will not be shaped by those who merely use AI.
It will be shaped by those who understand it deeply.

— Abeer & Amaara Verma

Preface

Why This Is a Master Guide
Artificial Intelligence is often discussed in fragments — one chapter on machine learning, another on ethics, another on automation.
But students need something different.

They need a structured, connected understanding of:
• What AI is
• How AI systems are built
• Where AI is applied
• How AI drives innovation
• What risks and responsibilities come with it
• How AI careers are evolving
AI Master Guide is designed as a complete student handbook — not just a collection of explanations.
It bridges:
Concept → Application → Innovation → Responsibility → Future Careers

Aligned with the spirit of NEP 2020 and 21st-century skill development, **this book encourages:**
• Systems thinking
• Analytical reasoning
• Ethical awareness
• Innovation mindset
• Entrepreneurial thinking
This guide is for students who want to move beyond curiosity and toward mastery.
Artificial Intelligence is powerful.
But informed students are more powerful.

Foreword

In We are entering a defining decade in technological history. Artificial Intelligence is reshaping industries, governance, research, and global economics at unprecedented speed. For the first time, students at the school level must engage with concepts that were once limited to advanced research institutions.

AI Master Guide responds to this need with clarity and structure. Rather than simplifying AI to the point of superficiality, it respects the intelligence of young learners while presenting concepts in an organized and accessible manner.

By combining technical insight with strategic and ethical reflection, Abeer and Amaara Verma offer a handbook that prepares students not only to understand AI — but to apply it responsibly and innovatively.

In a rapidly evolving digital economy, mastery will belong to those who:

- Understand systems
- Interpret data critically
- Innovate ethically
- Adapt continuously

This guide empowers students to move from awareness to competence — and from competence to innovation.
The future of AI will be written by informed minds.
This book is a step toward building them.

Contents

Chapter 1

What Is Artificial Intelligence?

The 5Ws for Curious Teens

Imagine having a friend who never sleeps, never forgets, and can answer almost anything in seconds. That's not a superhero—it's Artificial Intelligence, or AI. You may not realize it, but AI is already a part of your life. It helps you unlock your phone with your face, recommends your next favorite song, and even powers voice assistants like Alexa and Siri.

But what exactly is AI? How does it work? And why does it matter? In this chapter, we'll break it down using the 5Ws—What, Why, When, Where, and Who—to help you understand the basics of AI in the simplest, most exciting way possible.

What Is AI?

Artificial Intelligence (AI) is a branch of computer science that enables machines to think, learn, and make decisions—just like humans, but in a programmed way.

In simple words:
AI = A machine that learns from data and makes smart decisions. Unlike regular programs that follow strict instructions, AI systems can improve themselves by learning from experience. Think of AI as teaching a robot how to learn, not just how to follow.

Analogy: AI Is Like Training a Pet

Imagine you have a puppy. At first, it doesn't know anything. But if you show it enough times that "sit" means to sit, and you reward it with a treat, it learns. That's how AI works—

it needs:
- Input (like saying "sit")
- Data (rewards or corrections)
- Learning (over time, it gets better)

AI systems are trained using data in a similar way.

Why Do We Use AI?

The world is full of information—so much that humans alone can't manage it all.
AI helps us:
- Solve complex problems (like detecting diseases early)
- Save time (like suggesting email replies)
- Do repetitive tasks (like sorting millions of photos)
- Make the world smarter (smart homes, smart farming, smart assistants)

In short, we use AI to make life easier, faster, and more intelligent.

When Did AI Start?

You may think AI is something new, but it's been around since the 1950s!

• **1956 –** The term "Artificial Intelligence" was first used at a conference at Dartmouth College, USA.
• **1960s–80s –** Scientists developed simple computer programs that could play chess or solve math.
• **1997 –** IBM's AI computer Deep Blue beat world chess champion Garry Kasparov.
• **2000s–2020s –** AI exploded! With better internet, faster computers, and more data, AI started showing up in our daily lives—on phones, websites, cars, hospitals, and farms.

Now, we're in the AI revolution, and you're living right in the middle of it!

Where Is AI Used?

The real question is—where is AI NOT used? Here are just a few places you'll find AI:

Field	**Example**
Phones	Face unlock, voice assistants, autocorrect
Games	Enemies that learn your moves, smarter game bots
Shopping	Product recommendations on Amazon
Transport	Self-driving cars, smart traffic signals
Healthcare	AI that reads X-rays or predicts diseases
Farming	Drones that monitor crops, smart irrigation
Banking	Fraud detection, chatbots, loan approvals
Art & Music	AI that paints or composes songs
Education	Personalized learning apps, automatic grading

Did You Know?
AI can even help blind people "see" by describing surroundings using image recognition!

Who Works With AI?

AI is made by people—but not just computer engineers! It takes a team:

- AI Scientists & Researchers – design smart systems
- Data Scientists – clean and analyze data
- Software Developers – build AI-powered apps
- Psychologists – understand how humans think (to teach machines)
- Ethicists & Lawyers – ensure AI is fair and legal
- You! – Yes, even school students are creating AI projects!

In India, students as young as Grade 6 are learning about AI through CBSE & AI4Youth programs.

Try It Yourself!

Activity: "Where's the AI?"

List 5 things you did today that may have involved AI. Examples:

1. Used YouTube → AI recommends videos
2. Typed a message → AI autocorrects your spelling
3. Asked Alexa to play a song
4. Got Google Maps directions
5. Played an online game with smart bots

Can you find more?

Think & Reflect

"If AI can think and learn, does it have feelings or creativity like humans?"

Write your answer in 4–5 lines. Do you think AI should be treated like a human? Why or why not?

Career Corner: Future Jobs in AI

Here are some cool AI-related jobs of the future:

- AI Developer – Builds smart software
- Data Analyst – Finds patterns in data
- Ethical AI Specialist – Ensures fairness and privacy
- AI in Healthcare – Diagnoses patients or plans treatment
- Creative AI Designer – Creates AI-generated art or music
- AI Educator – Teaches people how to use AI safely

Many of these jobs didn't exist 10 years ago. That's the power of new technology!

Infographic Suggestion

Title: "The 5Ws of AI"

Design a colorful diagram with 5 circles connected to "AI" in the center:

- What – Smart machines that learn
- Why – To make life easier
- When – Since 1956, now everywhere
- Where – Phones, games, hospitals, farms
- Who – Scientists, students, even YOU

Use icons and simple visuals that explain each concept to a child.

Gamers' Corner

Did you ever notice that game characters get smarter the more you play?

That's AI! Game bots can learn your moves and change strategy.

AI also decides how difficult a game level should be based on your skill.

Next time you beat a level, thank your brain—and the game's brain too!

App Lab

Try This:
Go to https://teachablemachine.withgoogle.com
This is a free AI experiment where you can train your own model to

recognize:
- Your voice
- Your face
- Your gestures

It's like building your own mini AI. No coding needed!

Master Insight

Technical Lens (Abeer)
AI is not a single technology. It is an ecosystem of algorithms, data pipelines, and feedback systems working together.
Innovation Lens (Amaara)
When industries say they are "AI-powered," they are often redesigning entire systems — not just adding smart tools.

Summary

Let's wrap up the 5Ws of AI:
- What – AI means machines that learn, think, and decide
- Why – To solve problems, save time, and improve life
- When – Since the 1950s, now part of our everyday world
- Where – From classrooms to hospitals to shopping sites
- Who – Made by scientists, used by everyone—including YOU!

Chapter 2

How Does AI Work?

Understanding Data, Algorithms & Machine Learning – Made Simple

Have you ever wondered how AI knows your favorite song, or how Google Translate turns Hindi into English almost instantly? It's not magic—it's math, data, and learning.
In this chapter, we'll lift the curtain and explore how Artificial Intelligence actually works. Don't worry—we'll keep it fun and simple, like explaining it to a curious 12-year-old (because that's the point!).

We'll talk about:

- What is data?
- What are algorithms?
- What is machine learning?
- And how do they all work together to make AI smart?

What Is Data?

Data is the fuel that powers AI. It can be anything:

• Numbers
• Text
• Pictures
• Videos
• Sounds

When you post a selfie, that's data. When you rate a product 5 stars, that's data. Even your heart rate from a smartwatch is data.

AI needs a LOT of data to learn. The more it sees, the better it gets.

Fun Analogy: "Learning Like a Kid"

Imagine teaching a child what a "cat" looks like. You show them many photos of cats:
furry, whiskers, pointy ears.
Soon they can recognize one—even new ones!
AI learns the same way—by seeing many examples and finding patterns. It builds its understanding from data.

What Are Algorithms?

An algorithm is a step-by-step instruction for solving a problem.

Let's say you want to make Maggi. You follow a recipe:
1. Boil water
2. Add noodles
3. Add masala
4. Cook and stir

That's your Maggi algorithm!

AI uses similar instructions—but for computers. These algorithms tell AI how to look at data, compare patterns, and make decisions.

What Is Machine Learning?

Now comes the superhero of AI: Machine Learning (ML).
ML means teaching machines to learn from data—without being told everything.
Instead of programming each rule (like "if it has 4 legs and whiskers, it's a cat"), ML lets the machine figure it out from examples.
It's like saying:
"Here are 10,000 pictures of cats and dogs. Learn the difference by yourself."

Three Main Types of Machine Learning:

Type	What It Does	Example
Supervised Learning	Learns from labeled data	"This is a cat", "This is a dog"
Unsupervised Learning	Finds hidden patterns in unlabeled data	Groups of songs with similar rhythms
Reinforcement Learning	Learns from trial and error	Playing chess and getting better with wins/losses

Video game AI (like bots) uses reinforcement learning to get smarter every time you play!

How Do AI Systems Work Step-by-Step?

Let's look at a simplified AI Workflow:

1. Collect Data – Gather examples (photos, text, audio)
2. Clean Data – Remove mistakes, duplicates
3. Train the Model – Feed data into a machine learning algorithm
4. Test the Model – Check how well it learned
5. Deploy It – Use it in apps or websites
6. Improve Over Time – Feed new data to get smarter

Real-Life Example: AI That Recognizes Handwriting

Imagine an app that reads your handwriting:
1. It's shown thousands of handwritten letters (data)
2. It compares strokes, curves, and styles (algorithm)
3. It learns patterns of how "A" looks in many ways (machine learning)
4. Now it can read your own writing—even if it's messy!

Where You Already Use ML

You've already used machine learning without knowing it!

Examples:
- YouTube Recommendations – Learns what you watch
- Instagram Filters – Recognizes your face
- Google Maps – Learns traffic patterns
- Auto-Correct – Learns common typos and fixes them
- Spotify – Suggests songs based on your mood

Even Netflix uses ML to design posters just for you!

Analogy: Teaching a Robot to Tell Apples from Oranges

Here's a fun way to see how AI thinks:
Let's say you want to teach AI to know the difference between apples and oranges .
1. Collect Data: Take 1000 photos of apples and 1000 of oranges.
2. Train Model: Show them to the AI and label them.
3. AI Finds Patterns: Apples are red, round, smooth. Oranges are orange and bumpy.
4. Test: Show a new fruit and ask the AI: "Is this an apple or orange?"

5. AI Answers based on what it learned.
That's how image recognition AI works!

What Makes AI Smart?

AI becomes smarter when it has:

- Good Data – Clear, accurate, and diverse
- Powerful Computers – To process fast
- Feedback – Like tests and scores
- Human Help – We still guide AI to improve

Fun Fact: AI models are trained using supercomputers with GPUs (graphics processors) because they're fast at calculations.

Try It Yourself!

Activity: Create a Classifier with Teachable Machine

Visit: https://teachablemachine.withgoogle.com

1. Click "Get Started"
2. Choose "Image Project"
3. Create 2 classes (e.g., Happy Face vs Sad Face)
4. Use your webcam to record samples
5. Train the model
6. Try it live!

Now you've trained your own AI. No code needed!

Think & Reflect

If AI learns from examples, what happens if the examples are unfair or wrong?
Write your thoughts. For example, if you only show pictures of men as doctors, the AI might think only men can be doctors.
Why is it important to feed AI fair and balanced data?

Career Corner: Jobs That Understand "How AI Works"

If you enjoy how things work behind the scenes, here are exciting jobs:

- Machine Learning Engineer – Builds and trains AI models
- Data Scientist – Finds patterns and insights in data
- NLP Engineer – Works on voice and language AI (like Siri)
- AI Game Developer – Creates smart game characters
- AI Researcher – Studies how to make AI more intelligent

These jobs require curiosity, logic, and a love for solving puzzles!

Infographic Suggestion

Title: "How AI Learns – From Data to Decision"

Flowchart-style image showing:
Data → Algorithm → Machine Learning → Prediction/Decision → Feedback
Each step can be illustrated with a fun cartoon robot "learning" over time.

App Lab

Want to see ML in action?
Try the Google QuickDraw game: https://quickdraw.withgoogle.com
It asks you to draw things, and AI guesses what you're drawing in real-time—based on what millions of people drew before you.

Gamers' Corner

Did you know that AI in games learns your playing style?

In games like FIFA or Call of Duty, bots can:
- Learn your attack patterns
- Adjust their defense
- Even try to trick you

That's real-time learning—like a smart friend becoming a better competitor!

Master Insight

Technical Lens (Abeer)
The quality of an AI model depends more on data quality than algorithm complexity.
Innovation Lens (Amaara)
Poor data creates biased systems. Ethical innovation begins at the data collection stage.

Summary

Let's quickly recap how AI works:
- Data is the raw material – what the AI learns from
- Algorithms are the instructions – how it processes data
- Machine Learning is the method – how AI teaches itself
- Pattern recognition is key – AI spots trends
- Feedback loops make it smarter – the more it learns, the better it gets!

Now that you know how AI works, you're one step closer to building your own!

Chapter 3

AI in Daily Life

From Phones to Games to Shopping

You might think Artificial Intelligence (AI) is something far away—used in space missions or high-tech labs. But guess what?
AI is already in your hands, in your home, and even in your classroom.
From the moment you wake up and check your phone to the time you fall asleep listening to music, AI is quietly working in the background, making your life smoother, faster, and sometimes—more fun.
In this chapter, we'll explore how AI is part of our everyday lives—in gadgets, games, shopping, entertainment, and more!

Wake Up With AI

Let's walk through a typical day:

1. Morning Alarm – Your smart alarm app studies your sleep pattern and wakes you up at the best time.
2. Face Unlock – Your phone scans your face using AI-powered

facial recognition.
3. Weather App – Shows you today's forecast using AI prediction models.
4. News Feed – Curated just for you by AI, based on your reading history.
Even before breakfast, AI has already helped you four times!

AI in Music & Entertainment

Ever wonder how YouTube knows what to recommend next? Or how Spotify always seems to match your mood?

That's AI using pattern recognition and collaborative filtering:
- It learns what you like,
- Compares your tastes with others,
- And suggests content you'll probably enjoy.

AI Music Apps:
- Spotify – Suggests playlists using AI
- YouTube – Autoplays videos you might click
- Gaana, JioSaavn – Learn your musical language

AI even creates music now using tools like Amper or Soundraw!

Gamers' Corner

Yes, your video games are full of AI!

In games like:
- FIFA – Opponents learn your strategy
- Call of Duty – Bots adjust difficulty
- Minecraft – Mobs respond to your actions
- Chess Apps – Adapt to your level

These games use Reinforcement Learning, meaning the AI gets better by playing with you!

AI in Online Shopping

When you visit Amazon or Flipkart, you might notice:
• "Recommended for You" section
• Smart filters (price, size, color)
• Voice search ("Find blue sneakers")
• Chatbots helping with queries

That's e-commerce AI. It learns what you browse, when you buy, and what you ignore—then offers you better results.

AI is also used to:
• Manage inventory in warehouses
• Predict product demand
• Detect fake reviews

Real-Life Example: Smart Shopping Cart

Some stores in the U.S. and India now use AI-powered carts. You put items in the cart, and it:
• Scans them
• Adds prices
• Charges your account—without a cashier!
That's AI making shopping faster and touch-free.

AI in Cameras & Phones

Today's smartphones are super-smart—thanks to AI.

AI Camera Features:
• Scene recognition (sunset, food, pets)
• Portrait mode (blurs background like a DSLR)
• Smile & blink detection
• Auto-enhancement filters
• Night mode that brightens low light shots

Even Snapchat filters and Instagram AR masks are powered by AI face detection and movement tracking!

AI in Classrooms

You might be surprised—AI is already entering schools.

AI in Education:
• Personalized learning apps (like Byju's, Khan Academy)
• Auto-grading of quizzes
• AI tutors that adapt to your pace
• Speech-to-text for note-taking
• Translators for students in multilingual classes

CBSE's AI Curriculum now teaches AI from Grade 6!
India's AI for Youth program encourages students to create real-life AI projects.

AI in Homes: Smart Living

Smart homes use AI to make your surroundings intelligent.

Examples:
• Alexa, Siri, Google Assistant – Talk to devices!
• Smart Lights – Turn on when you walk in
• Smart Fridges – Suggest recipes based on food inside
• Voice Commands – "Play my playlist", "Switch off the fan"

AI helps save energy, increase comfort, and add fun.

AI on the Roads

AI helps cities and vehicles become safer and more efficient:
• Google Maps – Uses real-time traffic data
• Self-driving cars – Use AI to steer, brake, and park

• Smart traffic lights – Change based on car flow
• Toll booths – Scan license plates with AI vision

Even your driver's app (like Uber or Ola) uses AI to find routes, match drivers, and estimate fares.

Try It Yourself!

Activity: "Spot the AI Around You"
Make a list of 10 AI-powered things you used today.

Example:
1. Google Maps
2. Auto-correct in texting
3. Instagram filters
4. Shopping suggestions
5. YouTube autoplay

Tip: Ask your family—see how many they can name too!

Think & Reflect

AI makes our lives more convenient—but are we becoming too dependent?

Do you think people are losing skills because of AI? For example:
• Not memorizing phone numbers
• Not navigating without GPS
• Relying on autocorrect
Write your thoughts. Is it helpful, harmful, or a mix of both?

Career Corner: Jobs That Use AI in Daily Life

If you love apps, games, and gadgets, here are jobs where AI is used daily:

• Mobile App Developer – Builds smart phone features
• Game Designer – Uses AI for game logic
• Computer Vision Engineer – Makes smart cameras
• Chatbot Developer – Creates customer service bots
• UX Designer – Designs how people interact with AI tools

These careers mix tech + creativity—a great combo for future-ready students!

Infographic Suggestion

Title: "AI in a Day"

Create a visual timeline of a teen's day:
• Wake-up (AI alarm)
• Unlock phone (Face ID)
• Breakfast (Smart kitchen)
• School (AI tutor)
• Gaming (Smart bots)
• Instagram (AI filters)
• Online shopping
• Netflix (AI recommendations)
• Sleep tracker app

Use emojis, arrows, and icons to show where AI helps.

App Lab

Try Google Lens
• Open Google Lens on your phone
• Point it at a plant, a book, or a product
• It tells you what it is, where to buy, or what it means

That's AI-powered visual search!

Did You Know?

India has AI-powered robots like Mitra (used in banks and hospitals) that can:

- Recognize faces
- Speak multiple languages
- Guide customers

Mitra was even introduced to PM Modi and Ivanka Trump at an event!

Summary

Let's recap how AI is part of your daily life:

- Phones – Face ID, voice assistants, auto-correct
- Games – Smart bots and difficulty adjustment
- Shopping – Personalized suggestions and chatbots
- Music/Video – Recommendations tailored to your taste
- Classrooms – Smart tutors, quizzes, and translators
- Homes – Voice-activated devices and appliances
- Travel – Smart maps, route planning, toll scanning

AI isn't just in the future. It's already here—right in your pocket!

Chapter 4

Applications of AI Across Industries

Medicine, Education, Farming & More

Artificial Intelligence isn't just in your phone or games—it's powering some of the most important sectors of the world! From helping doctors diagnose diseases to supporting farmers in growing better crops, AI is becoming a behind-the-scenes hero.
In this chapter, let's explore how AI is being used across different fields—and how it's solving real problems in healthcare, education, agriculture, banking, environment, and even social media.

AI in Healthcare – Saving Lives with Smarts

AI is transforming how doctors and hospitals work.

What It Does:

• **Disease Detection:** AI scans X-rays and MRIs to find early signs of cancer, fractures, or infections.

• **Predictive Tools:** AI can predict disease outbreaks by analyzing health records and weather data.

- **Robot-Assisted Surgery:** Robots guided by AI can perform surgeries with precision.
- **Virtual Nurses:** Chatbots like “Molly” remind patients to take medicines.
- **COVID-19 Help:** AI tracked virus spread, managed vaccine distribution, and even screened symptoms using voice analysis.

India Example:
Startups like Niramai use AI to detect breast cancer early with thermal scans—non-invasive and affordable!

AI in Education – Smarter Classrooms

Learning isn’t one-size-fits-all. AI helps make education personal and interactive.

What It Does:
- **Smart Tutors:** Platforms like Byju’s, Khan Academy, and Toppr use AI to adapt lessons to student speed.
- **Automatic Grading:** AI checks objective questions and even short answers.
- **Voice-to-Text Tools:** Helpful for students with learning disabilities.
- **Language Translation:** Helps students learn in their mother tongue.
- **Attendance with Face Recognition:** Fast, contactless, and secure.

India Example:
The CBSE AI Curriculum teaches students how to build real AI projects using Scratch, Python, and Teachable Machine!

AI in Agriculture – Helping Farmers Grow Smarter

Farming is no longer just about hard work—it’s becoming high-tech with AI.

What It Does:

• **Crop Monitoring:** Drones and AI detect diseases, dryness, or pests in crops.

• **Smart Irrigation:** AI tells farmers when and how much to water.

• **Weather Forecasting:** AI predicts rainfall or drought more accurately.

• **Market Price Prediction:** Helps farmers decide the best time to sell.

• **Automated Harvesting:** AI-guided machines pick fruits and vegetables.

India Example:

The Ministry of Agriculture's Kisan AI platform helps farmers get advice in regional languages via voice AI.

AI in Governance – Smarter Public Services

Governments around the world are using AI to make services faster and fairer.

What It Does:

• **Traffic Management:** AI controls traffic lights based on real-time congestion.

• **Grievance Redressal:** AI sorts public complaints and sends them to the right departments.

• **Digital Identity:** Face and fingerprint recognition (like Aadhaar) use AI for authentication.

• **Crime Prediction:** AI helps analyze patterns to predict high-crime zones.

• **Judicial Assistance:** AI tools help judges review similar past cases faster.

India Example:

The Digital India Mission includes projects like eCourts and MyGov powered by AI chat assistants.

AI in Banking & Finance – Safer, Smarter Money

AI in finance helps keep your money safe—and your experience smooth.

What It Does:

- **Fraud Detection:** AI spots unusual transactions and blocks scams.
- **Chatbots:** Answer customer queries instantly (like HDFC's "Eva").
- **Loan Approval:** AI evaluates credit score and repayment history to give fair approvals.
- **Robo-Advisors:** Suggest where to invest based on your goals.
- **ATM Security:** Some ATMs now use AI facial recognition.

India Example:

ICICI Bank's AI chatbot iPal handles over 1 million customer queries every month—without human help!

AI in Transportation – Driving the Future

From ride apps to self-driving cars, AI is changing how we move.

What It Does:

- **Self-Driving Cars:** Use sensors and AI to steer, brake, and park.
- **Fleet Tracking:** AI tells delivery companies where trucks are and the best routes.
- **Predictive Maintenance:** AI alerts if a vehicle needs repairs soon.
- **Smart Ticketing:** Facial recognition for metro or bus entries.

India Example:

Bengaluru Metro is testing AI-based crowd control and facial-entry systems for contactless travel.

AI in Environment – Saving the Planet

AI helps us protect the Earth by monitoring, analyzing, and

responding to environmental changes.

What It Does:

- **Pollution Tracking:** AI studies air quality in cities and alerts people.
- **Wildlife Protection:** AI cameras detect poachers and endangered animals.
- **Forest Fire Prediction:** AI analyzes heat and dryness to warn early.
- **Waste Management:** AI robots sort garbage into recyclables and compost.
- **Water Clean-up:** AI robots help detect and remove plastic from rivers.

India Example:

AI tool Ganga Watch monitors water quality in the Ganga river using sensors and predictive analytics.

AI in Social Media – Behind the Scroll

Social media apps use AI more than you think.

What It Does:

- **Feed Personalization:** Shows you posts based on your behavior.
- **Hashtag Suggestions:** Based on trends and content.
- **Comment Moderation:** Blocks abusive or harmful content.
- **Face Tagging:** AI recognizes people in photos.
- **Ad Targeting:** You see ads that match your interests.

Caution: Social media AI can also create echo chambers—showing you only what you agree with.

AI in Art, Design & Creativity

Yes, AI can even paint, write poems, and make music!

What It Does:

- AI Art Tools: DALL•E and Canva's AI generate original pictures.

- **Music Generators:** AI composes melodies in seconds.
- **Writing Assistants:** AI helps draft stories or correct grammar.
- **Fashion Design:** AI predicts trends and suggests styles.
- **Interior Planning:** Suggests room layouts and furniture placement.

India Example:
Indian artists are using GANs (Generative Adversarial Networks) to create modern digital artwork for galleries.

Try It Yourself!

Activity: "Match the AI to the Industry"

Match the following industries with the AI tool:

Industry	AI Tool
Healthcare	a) Chatbot for banks
Education	b) Crop disease detector
Agriculture	c) Personalized tutor
Banking	d) Breast cancer scanner

Answers:
Healthcare → d
Education → c
Agriculture → b
Banking → a
Now try making your own examples!

Think & Reflect

"If AI is used everywhere, what happens if it makes a mistake?"
Imagine a misdiagnosis by a medical AI or a false accusation by crime-predicting software.

- Who should take responsibility?

• Should humans always be involved in final decisions?

Write your views. AI is powerful—but should it always be trusted?

Career Corner: Jobs in Industry AI

If you're curious about real-world problems and like solving them with tech, here are career options:

• AI in Healthcare – Medical AI Developer, Health Data Analyst
• AI in Education – EdTech AI Engineer, Learning App Designer
• AgriTech Expert – Drone-AI Developer, Precision Farming Analyst
• Finance AI Analyst – Risk Prediction Expert, Robo-Investment Designer
• Urban Planner – Uses AI for traffic, pollution, and safety models

These careers combine AI skills + real-world impact!

Infographic Suggestion

Title: "AI Across Industries"

Create a wheel or pie chart with each slice representing:

• Healthcare
• Education
• Agriculture
• Finance
• Transport
• Environment
• Art
• Social Media

Each section should show 2–3 icons and examples, with a central **label:** "AI is Everywhere!"

Master Insight

Technical Lens (Abeer)
Different industries require different model architectures — prediction models in finance differ from vision systems in healthcare.
Innovation Lens (Amaara)
AI innovation is most powerful when it solves localized problems, not just global trends.

Summary

Here's what we learned about AI applications:

- Healthcare – Diagnoses, robots, predictions
- Education – Smart tutors, translation, grading
- Agriculture – Drones, irrigation, weather AI
- Finance – Chatbots, fraud alerts, smart loans
- Transportation – Self-driving cars, GPS, ticketing
- Environment – Pollution control, fire alerts, waste sorting
- Social Media – Personalized feeds, content moderation
- Creativity – AI art, music, writing tools

AI is like electricity in the digital age—powering everything around us!

Chapter 5

How to Start Learning AI

(Even If You're a Teen)

You've learned what AI is, how it works, and how it's used in real life. Now comes the most exciting part—you can learn it too!
Yes, even if you're in Grade 6 or 12. You don't need to be a genius or know complex math. You just need curiosity, creativity, and a little bit of guidance.

This chapter is your step-by-step guide to begin your AI learning journey—with free tools, beginner-friendly platforms, fun activities, and simple code.

Step 1: Understand the Basics

Before you build AI, you should understand what it does:

- Recognize patterns (like cats vs dogs)
- Make decisions (like a chatbot replying)
- Predict outcomes (like which movie you'll like)
- Learn from data (like how you improve in a video game)

Start by reading simple articles or watching videos from:
• CBSE AI Curriculum YouTube
• Google AI for Youth India
• MIT Scratch AI Series

Pro Tip: Write down one new AI term you learn daily and explain it in your own words.

Step 2: Explore Beginner Tools – No Coding Needed!

There are many AI tools for beginners that require zero programming.

Try These:
1. Google Teachable Machine
Website: https://teachablemachine.withgoogle.com
What it does: Trains your computer to recognize images, sounds, or poses.
Example: Make it recognize your happy vs angry face using your webcam.

2. QuickDraw by Google
Website: https://quickdraw.withgoogle.com
What it does: You draw something, and AI guesses it in real-time.

3. Machine Learning for Kids
Website: https://machinelearningforkids.co.uk
What it does: Lets you train simple AI and connect it with Scratch to make games.

Step 3: Learn Block-Based Coding (If You're New to Code)

If you're just starting, go for drag-and-drop coding. It's fun and visual.

Start With:

- Scratch (scratch.mit.edu) – Make animations, stories, and games
- Code.org – Learn logic, loops, and fun games
- MIT App Inventor – Make your own apps without typing code

Example Project: Create a talking chatbot in Scratch that responds based on what the user types.

Gamers' Corner:

Build your own AI-powered rock-paper-scissors game with Scratch + ML.

Step 4: Move to Real Code (Optional, for Curious Teens)

If you're in Grades 8–12 and ready to try text-based programming, start with Python—the most popular language for AI.

Where to Start:

- Google Colab Notebooks – Free coding in browser
- Kaggle Datasets – Try small AI projects
- W3Schools Python Tutorial – Learn Python basics
- AI4ALL India – Indian youth-focused free courses

Learn basics first:

- Variables
- If-else conditions
- Loops
- Functions
- Arrays (lists)

Once comfortable, try libraries like TensorFlow or scikit-learn later.

Try It Yourself!

Activity: Make Your First AI Model
1. Visit: https://teachablemachine.withgoogle.com
2. Choose "Image Project"

3. Record 2 classes:
- o **Class 1:** You smiling
- o **Class 2:** You frowning

4. Train model
5. Test it live using webcam

Congratulations—you just created an AI model that recognizes emotions!

AI Learning Roadmap (Grade-Wise Guide)

Grade Level	Tools	Skills Focus
6–7	Scratch, Teachable Machine	Logic, creativity, basic AI ideas
8–9	MIT App Inventor, Code.org	Chatbots, voice commands, app design
10–12	Python, Google Colab, Kaggle	Real AI coding, datasets, model building

Tip: Make your learning social! Join AI clubs in school or form a coding group.

App Lab

Try these AI-friendly apps made for learners:
- AI Dungeon – Create stories with AI
- Canva AI – Use Magic Design to generate posters

• Replika – Chat with an AI bot
• Speechify – Text-to-speech for learning

Use them, explore how they work—and try to guess the AI behind the scenes!

Think & Reflect

If everyone can create AI, what kind of projects should you build? Should AI be used for fun only? Or also to solve real problems—like helping the blind, improving traffic, or saving water?
Write down 2 AI project ideas that can help your school, city, or family.

Career Corner: First Steps to Become an AI Professional

Even if you're a beginner, you're already on the path. Here are early roles for students:
• Student Innovator – Create AI projects for school or science fairs
• Junior Coder – Help your teacher or elder sibling with AI tools
• AI YouTuber – Create fun videos teaching AI tricks
• AI Storyteller – Use tools like ChatGPT to write books and comics
• AI Ethics Ambassador – Spread awareness on safe and fair AI

Bonus: Participate in national competitions like Intel AI4Youth, CBSE ATL Marathons, and Smart India Hackathon.

Infographic Suggestion

Title: "How to Start Learning AI – A Teen's Roadmap"

Create a flowchart with:
1. Curiosity
2. Use fun tools (Teachable Machine, Scratch)

3. Try mini-projects
4. Learn coding (Python)
5. Join contests
6. Build real-world AI ideas

Use arrows, emojis, and icons for each stage.

Did You Know?

The youngest AI developer in India, Tanmay Bakshi, started coding at age 5 and built his first AI project at age 12. Now he's helping companies like IBM!

Summary

Let's review how you can start learning AI:

- Begin with curiosity and simple tools (like Teachable Machine)
- Use block-based platforms (Scratch, App Inventor) to make games or chatbots
- Move to Python when ready to build real AI models
- Join competitions and communities to grow
- Keep exploring—because AI is a journey, not a destination!

You don't need to know everything. Just start. Ask questions. Try something new. That's the real magic of AI.

Chapter 6

AI vs Human Intelligence

Myths & Truths

Can AI think like a human? Will robots replace teachers or doctors? Will AI become smarter than us?

These are common questions—and sometimes fears—about Artificial Intelligence. But the truth is, while AI is powerful, it's very different from human intelligence.

In this chapter, we'll separate facts from fiction, bust some popular myths, and understand what AI can and cannot do.

Let's dive into the world of machine vs mind!

What Is Human Intelligence?

Human intelligence is the ability to:

- Learn from experience
- Think creatively and emotionally
- Solve new problems
- Understand context and meaning
- Show empathy, values, and imagination

You don't just follow rules—you make decisions using your feelings, memories, ethics, and even your gut!

Example:
When you see your friend is sad, you might not say anything logical—you give a hug. That's human connection. AI can't feel that.

What Is Artificial Intelligence?

AI is created by humans to:
- Recognize patterns
- Process large amounts of data
- Perform specific tasks
- Learn through data (not emotions)
- Predict outcomes based on past input

AI doesn't "think" like a human. It simulates intelligence—but doesn't understand or feel.

It's a tool, not a being.

AI vs Human Brain: Key Differences

Feature	**Human Brain**	**AI**
Learning	From experience & emotions	From data only
Creativity	Imagination, art, innovation	Mimics patterns
Emotion	Feels love, sadness, empathy	Has none
General Thinking	Solves new problems	Needs training for each task
Decision-making	Moral, ethical, situational	Based on logic or data
Energy	20 watts (efficient)	Needs powerful computers

Flexibility	Can switch tasks easily	Limited to one task at a time

Myth Buster Zone

Myth 1: "AI can think like humans."
Truth:
AI can mimic how humans talk or behave, but it doesn't understand emotions, context, or morality. For example, a chatbot may say "I'm sorry" but doesn't feel sorry.

Myth 2: "AI will take over the world."
Truth:
AI has no goals or ambition. It doesn't want to rule. It's a tool used by humans. The real danger is not AI—but how humans use it. Responsibility matters!

Myth 3: "Robots will replace all jobs."
Truth:
Yes, some routine jobs will change. But new jobs are also being created—like AI Ethics Officer, AI Trainers, Data Curators, etc. Human creativity, leadership, and emotional intelligence are still irreplaceable.

Myth 4: "AI is always accurate."
Truth:
AI can make mistakes—especially if trained with bad or biased data. That's why human supervision is still important.

Real-Life Example: Chess Champion vs AI
In 1997, IBM's AI system Deep Blue defeated world chess champion Garry Kasparov. AI could calculate millions of moves per second—but Kasparov used intuition and experience.
Even today, humans and AI work best together:
Human + AI = Superpower!

Can AI Be Creative?

Yes… and no.

AI tools like:

• DALL•E – Create pictures from text
• ChatGPT – Write poems or scripts
• Jukebox AI – Compose music

They look creative—but they're really combining what they've seen before. They don't "feel" art or "invent" new ideas from nothing. Humans create from emotion. AI creates from data.

When AI Imitates Humans…

Sometimes AI feels human:

• Voice assistants talk like us
• Chatbots answer like us
• Virtual influencers exist on Instagram

But it's just imitation, not intelligence.
Just because it looks real, doesn't mean it understands.

Example: A talking parrot copies words, but doesn't know what "I love you" means.

Did You Know?

AI once wrote an article for a major newspaper saying "I come in peace" to convince readers it had no desire to harm humans. It sounded real—but was completely generated using patterns.

Think & Reflect

If AI can't feel or understand the world like humans, should it ever make important decisions—like hiring people or judging court cases? Should humans always have the final say?
Write your view. Think about fairness, bias, and emotion.

Try It Yourself!

Activity: Human or AI?
Search for 3 pieces of content online—a painting, a poem, and a song.
Can you guess if each one was created by a human or by AI?
Hint: Use tools like This Person Does Not Exist, DALL•E, or AI art apps to explore creations.

Then ask: does knowing the creator change how you feel about it?

Ethics Matter: Who's Responsible?

If an AI system makes a mistake (e.g., arrests the wrong person), who should be blamed?
• The company who built it?
• The person who used it?
• The coder who trained it?
These are real questions being debated worldwide.
That's why AI needs ethical rules—just like we have laws.

Career Corner: Jobs at the Human-AI Intersection

Love both tech and people? These future roles are for you:
• AI Ethics Officer – Ensures fairness and safety
• AI Educator – Helps others understand AI
• Cognitive Scientist – Studies human vs machine learning
• Human-AI Interaction Designer – Builds AI that works well with people
• AI Policy Maker – Creates laws for AI use
The best AI future is not just about coding—but caring, questioning, and guiding it.

Infographic Suggestion

Title: "AI vs Human Intelligence – What's the Difference?"

Design two side-by-side columns:

- Brain icon for humans
- Robot head icon for AI

Under each, list traits:

- Feels emotions vs no emotion
- General thinker vs specific task
- Learns creatively vs from data
- Makes ethical choices vs only logic

Use color coding and emojis for visual clarity.

App Lab

Try Replika AI (a chatbot friend).

Chat with it for 5 minutes and note:

- Does it feel real?
- Does it understand your feelings?

Then compare it to a chat with your real friend or sibling. What's different?

Master Insight

Technical Lens (Abeer)
Automation scales efficiency — but poorly designed automation scales errors just as fast.
Innovation Lens (Amaara)
Organizations that automate responsibly gain trust. Those that automate blindly risk reputational damage.

Summary

Let's clear up what AI is—and isn't:

- AI is smart, but not human
- It's great at data and patterns, not emotions
- AI doesn't "think" or "feel"—it predicts
- Humans have empathy, ethics, and intuition
- AI can assist—but shouldn't replace—human judgment

The truth? AI is powerful, but it needs people like YOU to use it wisely.

Chapter 7

Ethics, Safety, and Digital Responsibility

Using AI the Right Way

Artificial Intelligence is powerful—and like any powerful tool, it must be used with care.

Think of fire: it can cook your food, but it can also burn down a house. The same goes for AI. It can help blind people "see" or spread fake news. It can assist in exams—or help someone cheat.
That's why, as future creators and users of AI, you must understand ethics, safety, and digital responsibility.
This chapter will guide you through what's right, what's risky, and what you can do to stay smart and safe in an AI-powered world.

What Is AI Ethics?

Ethics means knowing the difference between right and wrong.

AI Ethics is about making sure AI:
•Is fair and unbiased

• Protects privacy
• Respects human rights
• Doesn't harm people
• Is used for good, not evil

Just because something can be done with AI, doesn't mean it should be.

What Can Go Wrong With AI?

Let's look at some real dangers if AI is misused or poorly designed:

1. Bias in AI

If an AI is trained on unfair data (e.g., only male doctors, only white faces), it may:
• Reject job applicants unfairly
• Misidentify people from certain backgrounds
• Promote harmful stereotypes

Real Example: Some facial recognition systems were found to be less accurate for women and people with dark skin.

2. Loss of Privacy

AI collects and analyzes lots of data:
• Location
• Search history
• Voice recordings
• Face or fingerprints

Without consent, this becomes a privacy invasion.

Tip: Always check app permissions before clicking "Allow".

3. Deepfakes & Fake Content

AI can now create:
- Fake voices
- Fake videos (deepfakes)
- Fake news articles

These can be used to:
- Spread misinformation
- Scam people
- Defame someone's image

Did You Know?
Deepfake videos have been used to show politicians saying things they never said!

4. Cheating & Overdependence

Some students use AI to:
- Write assignments
- Pass online exams
- Create fake projects

This harms real learning and growth.

Learning with AI is great—but letting AI do everything weakens your thinking skills.

AI & YOU: Digital Responsibility

As a student and digital citizen, you play a role in using AI wisely.

Here's your AI Code of Conduct:
DO:
- Use AI to learn and create

- Question how an AI system works
- Report harmful or fake content
- Protect your data and passwords
- Encourage fairness and inclusivity

DON'T:

- Use AI to cheat
- Spread AI-generated lies
- Bully others using anonymous tools
- Copy art or text without credit
- Share personal data carelessly

Being ethical means making choices that are safe, kind, and smart.

Try It Yourself!

Activity: "Create Your AI Code of Honor"
Write your own 5-rule "AI Code of Honor" as a future AI creator or user.

For example:

1. I will not use AI to lie or hurt others.
2. I will respect data privacy.
3. I will learn, not cheat.
4. I will report misuse.
5. I will teach others how to be safe with AI.

Hang it by your study desk or share with your school AI club!

Think & Reflect

If an AI system does something wrong—like blocks your account or gives you wrong marks—should you be able to question it?
Who decides what's fair: the AI or a human?
Write down how you would feel, and what rules you think every AI system should follow.

Career Corner: Be a Responsible AI Leader

Interested in the human side of tech?

Here are ethical AI roles:

- AI Ethics Researcher – Studies fairness and impact of AI
- Tech Policy Advisor – Works with governments to create AI laws
- AI Ethics Educator – Teaches AI responsibility in schools
- Bias Tester – Finds errors in how AI makes decisions
- AI Rights Activist – Promotes inclusive and kind AI systems

The future needs not just coders—but ethical leaders in AI!

What Are the 5 Pillars of Responsible AI?

These are the international golden rules for ethical AI:

Pillar	**Meaning**
Fairness	No discrimination or bias
Privacy	Data must be protected
Transparency	People should know how AI works
Accountability	Someone must be responsible
Safety	AI should not cause harm

Many countries, including India, follow these principles in their AI policies.

How to Spot Fake AI Content

Tips to Detect Deepfakes or AI Scams:

- Check if the voice sounds robotic or mismatched
- Look at the eyes and mouth in videos—do they blink oddly?
- Google reverse image search to see if a photo is fake

• Be suspicious of WhatsApp forwards or too-good-to-be-true news
If unsure—don't share.

India's Digital Safety Initiatives

India is taking big steps to protect people in the AI age:
• Digital India Act – Updating laws for online safety
• NITI Aayog's Responsible AI Guidelines – For fair and inclusive AI
• CyberSafe India Program – Trains school children in online ethics
• Bhashini AI Mission – Promotes multilingual, ethical AI tools
You can join awareness campaigns or become a Digital Safety Ambassador in your school!

Infographic Suggestion

Title: "AI Safety Do's & Don'ts"
Design a poster with two columns:

Do's
• Learn with AI
• Use it kindly
• Question its logic
• Share responsibly

Don'ts
• Use AI to cheat
• Share deepfakes
• Break privacy
• Trust blindly

Add icons like locks, warning signs, and smiley faces for visual impact.

App Lab

Try the app Zigazoo Kids – a safe, moderated platform that uses AI to filter harmful comments and promote positive conversations. Explore how AI moderation works—and suggest ideas to make it even safer!

Summary

Here's how to use AI the right way:

- Be aware of risks like bias, privacy loss, and fake content
- Be responsible while using or creating AI tools
- Be ethical—choose kindness, truth, and fairness
- Be informed—understand how AI decisions are made
- Be a role model—teach others safe AI habits

AI is not just about technology—it's about values. And with great power comes great responsibility.

Chapter 8

AI for Good

Solving Real Problems

What if we told you that AI could save lives, clean oceans, teach kids, and help the blind see?

Sounds like a superhero, right?
In this chapter, we'll discover the good side of Artificial Intelligence—how it is being used to solve real-world challenges, especially in India and developing countries. From healthcare to disaster response, AI is helping humanity in ways never imagined. Because when AI is used with purpose, it becomes a powerful tool for progress.

AI for the Environment

1. Cleaning Rivers and Oceans
Plastic pollution in rivers like the Ganga and Yamuna is a big problem.

AI-powered robots like "WasteShark" or Nudges.ai can:
• Detect and collect floating plastic
• Track pollution levels using satellite images
• Suggest cleanup routes for faster action

In India, startups use AI to:
• Monitor Ganga water quality
• Alert authorities about chemical leaks
• Analyze satellite images for illegal dumping

2. Predicting Natural Disasters
AI tools can analyze weather, soil, satellite data to predict:
• Floods
• Earthquakes
• Cyclones
• Forest fires
NASA and ISRO use AI models to provide early warnings.

In Bihar and Assam, AI apps warn villagers about flooding hours in advance—saving lives and crops!

AI for Healthcare Access

AI is making healthcare affordable and reachable, even in remote areas.

Real-World Uses:
• AI Chatbots like "mFine" or Ada ask patients questions and suggest possible health conditions
• AI Eye Scans detect blindness early—used by Aravind Eye Hospital in India
• Mobile X-Ray AI tools detect pneumonia and TB in seconds
• Drone Deliveries send medicine and vaccines to hilly or tribal villages

These tools save time, cost, and lives—especially in places with few doctors.

AI for Mental Health & Disabilities

AI is helping people feel seen and heard—even those struggling silently.

Tools That Care:

- Wysa – An Indian mental health chatbot that gives emotional support
- Voice AI – Detects depression or anxiety based on speech patterns
- Image-to-Text AI – Helps blind users read printed documents
- Sign Language AI – Converts gestures into text or voice for deaf users

AI is not replacing doctors—it's supporting them to reach more people faster.

AI for Quality Education

Millions of children miss out on good education. AI helps bridge that gap.

AI in Education for Good:

- Personalized Learning – Adapts content based on student's speed
- Translation Tools – Make lessons available in 22+ Indian languages
- Accessibility Features – Read-aloud tools, enlarged text, subtitles
- Offline AI Tools – Work without internet in tribal or rural schools

Projects like Google's Bolo (now Read Along) teach rural kids to read in Hindi and English using voice AI!

AI in Smart Farming

Many Indian farmers face losses due to unpredictable weather or pests.
AI helps improve crop yield, reduce waste, and increase income.

AI on the Field:

- Kisan AI Voice Assistants – Help farmers get weather or market updates
- Crop Disease Detection – Phone cameras + AI detect early signs
- Soil Testing AI – Suggests fertilizers based on land condition
- Supply Chain AI – Connects farmers directly with buyers, reducing middlemen

Example: Microsoft partnered with ICRISAT to build an AI tool that predicts the best sowing dates using weather and soil data.

AI for Social Justice

AI can also fight inequality and support justice systems.

How?

- Analyzing large volumes of legal cases to support faster judgments
- Predicting which areas need more policing or social support
- Voice AI apps to help marginalized communities report abuse
- AI bots to translate legal help into regional languages

In India, the Jugalbandi Project uses WhatsApp + AI to provide villagers access to government schemes in their language.

Try It Yourself!

Activity: Dream an AI for Good
Imagine a problem in your school, town, or city.
Now design an AI tool to solve it.

Answer:

1. What is the problem?
2. Who will use your AI?
3. What data will it need?
4. What will it do?

Example:

Problem – Food waste in your canteen
AI Tool – Smart camera that counts leftover food daily
Impact – Suggests changes in meal planning

Think & Reflect

Should all AI projects aim to help society?
Some AI is made only for money or entertainment. But could every

AI project have a positive impact?
Can you think of ways to turn fun AI (like chatbots or filters) into tools that help people?

Career Corner: Be an AI Changemaker

Want to build tech for good? Explore these roles:

- AI for Environment Specialist – Builds tools to fight climate change
- Inclusive AI Designer – Makes tools accessible for all backgrounds
- Data for Good Analyst – Uses data to solve social problems
- Education Tech Developer – Builds learning apps for rural kids
- AI Policy Consultant – Works with governments for ethical innovation

Join NGOs, school projects, or local hackathons that focus on social impact through AI!

Global Examples of AI for Good

• UNICEF's AI for Children – Promotes child rights through responsible AI
• Wildbook AI – Tracks endangered animals by their photos
• Plantix App – Helps farmers in India detect pests using AI
• Seeing AI by Microsoft – Describes the world to blind users in real-time
• Disaster Alert AI – Predicts and maps natural disasters worldwide
These projects prove AI is not just smart—it can be kind.

Infographic Suggestion

Title: "AI for Good – Real Impact Around Us"

Create icons for each category:

- Healthcare
- Agriculture
- Education
- Environment
- Mental Health
- Social Justice

Next to each icon, add 1 real example (e.g., Wysa for mental health, Bolo for reading, CropIn for farming).

App Lab

Try the Google Read Along (Bolo) app.

It uses speech recognition to:

• Help kids read aloud
• Give instant feedback
• Work offline in Indian languages

Test how it helps a younger sibling—or yourself. Could you build something similar?

Master Insight

Technical Lens (Abeer)
Algorithmic transparency is not optional. Systems must be auditable and explainable.
Innovation Lens (Amaara)
Ethics is no longer a compliance requirement — it is a competitive advantage.

Summary

Let's celebrate how AI is being used for good:

- Helps doctors, teachers, farmers, and children
- Protects the planet, predicts disasters
- Supports mental health and the disabled
- Promotes fairness, justice, and inclusion
- Bridges digital gaps in rural India

AI is more than coding and gadgets—it's a chance to build a better world.
And it starts with young changemakers like you.

Chapter 9

Cool Projects You Can Try

From Chatbots to AI Art

Want to make your own AI project?
You don't need to be a tech genius or wait till college. With the right tools and a little creativity, you can start building AI projects right now—even in school!
This chapter is full of exciting, beginner-friendly AI projects you can try using simple platforms like Scratch, Teachable Machine, Google Colab, and Canva AI.
Let's create something fun, meaningful, and truly yours!

Project 1: Make Your Own Chatbot

What It Does:
A chatbot is a mini robot that talks to users. It can answer questions, have simple conversations, or guide people.

Tools:
- Scratch + Machine Learning Extension

• Dialogflow (by Google)
• MIT App Inventor

Steps:
1. Choose a topic: e.g., Study Buddy, Mood Bot, or Homework Helper
2. Create responses for different questions
3. Add logic: "If the user says X, bot replies Y"
4. Test your chatbot with friends!

Tip: Use voice input features to make it speak like Siri!

Project 2: AI That Recognizes Emotions

What It Does:
Teaches your computer to read your facial expressions and label your mood.

Tool:
• Google Teachable Machine

Steps:
1. Open Teachable Machine > Image Project
2. Record 3 moods (happy, sad, angry) using your webcam
3. Train your model
4. Test it in real time

Add it to a story app where the background changes based on your mood!

Project 3: Create AI-Generated Art

What It Does:
Turn words into art using AI.

Tools:
• DALL•E
• Craiyon
• Canva AI Art Generator

Steps:
1. Go to DALL•E or Canva
2. Type a prompt like: "An astronaut riding a tiger through space in Van Gogh style"
3. Watch your art come alive!
4. Print it as posters, bookmarks, or notebook covers.

Tip: Make a mini art gallery at school with "Created by AI" tags!

Project 4: Rock-Paper-Scissors Game with AI

What It Does:
Play the game using your hand gestures and AI will recognize your move.

Tools:
• Teachable Machine
• Scratch + Webcam Extension

Steps:
1. Record your hand showing Rock, Paper, Scissors
2. Train your model
3. Connect it to Scratch so the computer plays back
4. Add scoring and fun sound effects!
You now have a smart game bot that sees your hands!

Project 5: Smart Quiz App

What It Does:
A quiz app that gives you questions based on your level.

Tools:
• MIT App Inventor
• Google Sheets (for question storage)
• Voiceflow or Dialogflow (for smart voice features)

Steps:
1. Build a quiz format
2. Add AI that checks your previous score
3. Adjust the question difficulty
4. Include text-to-speech so it can read questions aloud!

Bonus: Add a "Fun Fact" after every answer to make it more educational.

Project 6: Object Detection Game

What It Does:
Recognizes real-world objects like pens, bottles, books using your webcam.

Tools:
• Google Teachable Machine
• Webcam + HTML/CSS if advanced

Steps:
1. Record images of your real items
2. Train the model to label them
3. **Add scoring:** "Find and show 3 items in 30 seconds"
4. Timer counts your object match speed

Great for a classroom **"AI Treasure Hunt"** activity!

Project 7: AI Poetry Generator

What It Does:
Generates random poems or jokes using your input.

Tools:
- ChatGPT Playground (for advanced users)
- Scratch or Google Forms + Response AI

Steps:
1. Ask the user to enter a mood: "happy, sad, silly"
2. Generate a short poem or quote
3. Display it with fun colors and fonts

Tip: Compile a poetry e-book made by "AI + Me".

Project 8: Voice-Controlled Assistant (Like Mini-Alexa)

What It Does:
Responds to voice commands like "What's the time?" or "Tell a joke!"

Tools:
- Voiceflow
- Dialogflow
- Python + SpeechRecognition (advanced)

Steps:
1. Record voice commands
2. Create matching responses
3. Add smart actions like showing a clock, playing music, etc.
4. Use a speaker to make it interactive

Test it with your friends and say "Hi AI!"

App Lab

Try MIT App Inventor to build your own AI-powered Android apps. Free, drag-and-drop blocks, and even includes camera, voice, and sensors.

Project ideas:
• Mood Tracker App
• Plant Care Reminder with Voice Alerts
• Language Quiz Bot

Publish your app and show off at school exhibitions!

Try It Yourself!

Activity: Design Your Dream AI Project

Answer these to get started:
1. What will your AI do?
2. Who will it help?
3. What data will it need?
4. What platform/tool will you use?
5. What will make it unique?

Draw or sketch your app screen, chatbot face, or game layout. Present your idea to your class and vote on the coolest one!

Think & Reflect

Should AI projects always be fun, or should they also solve problems?
Can you mix both?
Write down 1 idea for a fun + helpful AI tool. Example: A voice bot that tells jokes and helps reduce stress!

Career Corner: From School Projects to Startups

Today's student AI project could become tomorrow's startup.

Careers to explore:

- AI Product Designer – Builds fun tools people love
- EdTech Developer – Makes AI games for learning
- AI Game Designer – Codes smart characters
- Creative Technologist – Mixes AI and design
- Conversational AI Developer – Builds chatbots and voice bots

Tip: Share your projects on GitHub or participate in student hackathons like:

- CBSE ATL Marathon
- AI4Youth India
- Technovation Girls
- Codeavour International AI Challenge

Infographic Suggestion

Title: "Cool AI Projects for Students"

Create a poster layout with icons:

- Chatbot
- AI Art
- AI Game
- Voice Assistant
- Quiz App
- Poem Generator

Add **"Tools You Can Use"** section: Teachable Machine, Scratch, App Inventor, Canva, Voiceflow

Master Insight

Technical Lens (Abeer)
Rapid prototyping with AI APIs allows students to build functional MVPs without full-scale infrastructure.
Innovation Lens (Amaara)
Innovation is not about using AI everywhere — it is about identifying where AI adds meaningful value.

Summary

Let's review what you can create:
• Chatbots to answer or entertain
• Games that recognize hand gestures
• Apps that quiz or teach
• Art that starts with just a sentence
• Projects that combine voice, vision, and logic

The best part? You don't need to wait. You can start today.
With your imagination and the tools around you, you are the future of AI.

Chapter 10

AI & The Future of Work

Jobs, Skills & Opportunities

"Will robots take our jobs?"
This is one of the most asked questions about Artificial Intelligence.
The answer is both yes and no.
Yes, AI will change how we work.
No, it won't take away all jobs—instead, it will create new ones and change the skills we need.
In this chapter, we'll explore how AI is shaping the future of work, what jobs will disappear, what new roles will emerge, and what skills students need to be future-ready.

Jobs AI Might Replace

AI is great at repetitive, rule-based tasks. So, jobs that require repetition and no creativity may be automated.

At Risk:

• Data entry operators

• Bank clerks
• Call center agents
• Cashiers
• Ticket booking staff
• Basic factory line workers

These roles may shrink because AI and robots can do them faster and without breaks.

Jobs AI Will Create

For every job AI replaces, it creates new ones that never existed before.

Emerging AI-Powered Careers:
• Machine Learning Engineer
• Data Scientist
• AI Ethics Consultant
• Game AI Developer
• Robotics Technician
• AI Trainer (teaches AI using data)
• Chatbot Designer
• AI Art Creator
• Predictive Analyst
• AI in Healthcare Specialist

Many of these careers need human + AI teamwork!

Jobs That Will Transform

Some jobs won't disappear—but they'll change with AI tools.

Career	Old Style	AI-Enhanced
Teacher	Blackboard teaching	Personalized AI apps

Doctor	Manual diagnosis	AI-assisted imaging
Farmer	Guesswork on weather	AI-based irrigation
Banker	Manual checks	Robo-advisors
Artist	Paint & canvas	AI-assisted design

In the future, AI won't replace you—it will empower you (if you know how to use it).

AI in Different Industries

Healthcare:
• Disease prediction, drug development, AI-assisted surgery

Education:
• Smart tutors, content creation, learning analytics

Finance:
• Fraud detection, robo-investments, customer chatbots

Manufacturing:
• Quality control using vision AI, smart robots

Law:
• AI to review past judgments, assist legal research

Food:
• Smart recipe generators, kitchen robots (like Nosh)

Future-Proof Skills You Should Learn

You don't need to be a coder to succeed in the AI future. But you do need:

Top 10 Skills:

1. Problem-solving
2. Critical thinking
3. Creativity
4. Communication
5. Emotional intelligence
6. Collaboration
7. Digital literacy
8. Data awareness
9. Ethics and responsibility
10. Curiosity and learning mindset

AI is just a tool—the real skill is how you use it.

Try It Yourself!

Activity: "Design Your Future Job"
Imagine it's 2035. You're working in an AI-powered world.

Fill this out:
- Job Title: ____________________
- What do you do daily?
- What AI tools help you?
- What human skills do you use?
- How does your job help people?

Example:
Job Title: Emotional AI Coach
Daily Work: Teach robots to recognize emotions
Tools: Facial AI, empathy models
Skills: Psychology + tech
Impact: Helps AI communicate with kindness

Think & Reflect

Should students focus only on coding to prepare for the AI future?
Can storytellers, teachers, or sports coaches also be part of the AI world?
Write your view. List 2 non-tech jobs that could use AI in the future.

Future Career Paths – Streams + AI

School Stream	AI-Linked Career
Science	AI Researcher, Bioinformatics Analyst
Commerce	FinTech Analyst, AI Business Strategist
Humanities	AI Ethics Officer, Linguistic AI Trainer
Arts	AI Illustrator, Game Narrative Designer
Vocational	Robotics Assembler, Drone Technician

No matter what stream you choose—AI has a place in your journey.

App Lab

Try TCS iON Career Insight – An Indian platform that uses AI to guide students based on their interests, skills, and career preferences. Take a quiz and explore AI-powered jobs that match your personality!

What Companies Want in Future Employees

Big employers are already looking for:

- People who can work with AI tools
- Team players who can collaborate with machines and humans
- Ethical thinkers who use AI responsibly
- Lifelong learners who adapt to new tech quickly

Tip: Start building your portfolio now—projects, apps, writing, videos, designs.

What Will Work Look Like in 2040?

Imagine:
- Global teams with AI translators
- Smart glasses showing real-time data
- Factory robots managed by voice
- Virtual teachers powered by AI
- Managers using AI dashboards to track wellness

The office of the future will be digital, flexible, and intelligent. Will you be ready?

Infographic Suggestion

Title: "AI + Careers = Your Future"

Show 3 categories:
- Jobs AI will change (with icons)
- Jobs AI will create (with new job titles)
- Skills you need (icons for soft + tech skills)

Use arrows and future-themed illustrations like robots in lab coats, AI glasses, smart classrooms.

Did You Know?

According to the World Economic Forum:
- 85 million jobs may be displaced by automation
- But 97 million new roles will be created!

It's not about losing jobs—it's about changing jobs.

Summary

Let's review the future of work with AI:

- Some jobs will be automated
- Many will transform and need new tools
- Entirely new careers will emerge
- Human skills like empathy and creativity will shine
- Students from every stream can enter the AI workforce

The best way to prepare?

Stay curious, keep learning, and use AI as your partner—not your replacement.

Chapter 11

Girls & Boys in AI

Let's All Join In!

When you think of AI scientists or tech experts, who comes to mind? A man in a lab coat? A male coder in glasses?

That's a stereotype. And it's time to change it.
Artificial Intelligence is for everyone—girls, boys, rural kids, city kids, artists, gamers, writers, and scientists.

In this chapter, we'll explore how students from all backgrounds and genders can join the world of AI—and why diversity makes AI better.

Why Inclusivity Matters in AI

If only one kind of person creates AI, the results will be one-sided.

Problem:

- AI may ignore other cultures, languages, or needs

• AI may show bias (e.g., show only male doctors in search results)
• AI may not work well for people with disabilities or different skin tones

Solution:
We need people of all genders, regions, languages, and abilities to design AI that works for everyone.

The more voices in AI, the smarter and fairer it becomes.

Breaking Barriers: Challenges Girls Often Face in Tech

In many places, girls are underrepresented in AI and coding clubs.

Why?
• Fewer role models
• Lack of tech access
• Social pressure ("Tech is for boys")
• Less confidence (even when equally talented!)

But this is changing—fast.

Inspiring Girls in AI – Real Role Models

1. Tanya Notley (Australia)
Created AI workshops for teen girls to learn ethics and build their own chatbots.

2. Shweta Rawat (India)
Built an AI tool for early detection of cervical cancer in rural India.

3. Avye Couloute (UK, started at age 11!)
Builds AI-powered robots and runs coding workshops for girls.

4. Riya Bansal (India)
Won CBSE's ATL Marathon for creating a Teachable Machine-based disaster alert system.

These girls didn't wait to grow up—they started early, just like you can!

Boys as Allies in Inclusion

Boys play a powerful role in making the tech world inclusive.

How?
• Share resources and encourage peers of all genders
• Break gender stereotypes in your group
• Form mixed AI teams for school projects
• Speak up if someone says "girls can't code" (that's false!)
Tech is better when everyone contributes.

Programs Empowering Girls in AI

1. Technovation Girls
Global challenge where girls build AI-powered apps for real-world problems.

2. SheCodes India
Workshops and scholarships for coding and AI education.

3. CBSE ATL Tinkerpreneur
Encourages innovation from both girls and boys across India.

4. Girls Who Code
Free resources, clubs, and sisterhood for girls in tech.

School Ideas to Promote Gender Equity in AI

- Start AI Clubs that actively invite everyone to join
- Display posters of diverse role models
- Host mixed-gender AI project fairs
- Offer equal access to devices during coding time
- Include female mentors and guest speakers in AI sessions

Equality starts in your classroom.

Try It Yourself!

Activity: "Interview a Future AI Leader"
Pick a classmate of the opposite gender. Interview them!

Questions:
- What do you like about AI?
- What would you build with AI?
- Who inspires you?
- What do you want others to know about your journey?

Write and present their story as an **"AI Hero Spotlight."**

Think & Reflect

If only boys built all the AI, what problems might get ignored?
If only girls did, what perspectives might be missing?
Why is it important that people from different genders and backgrounds work together?

Write your opinion and share it during an AI Club discussion.

Career Corner: Inclusive AI Careers

Diverse teams are in high demand in these careers:
- AI Product Tester – Makes sure AI works for all users

• Game Narrative Designer – Builds inclusive characters and stories
• UX Designer – Designs apps for all genders and age groups
• AI Fairness Consultant – Checks if AI treats everyone equally
• AI Mentor – Helps rural and urban youth access tech skills

You don't just build AI—you build a better world with it.

Infographic Suggestion

Title: "AI Is for Everyone"

Show a group of kids:
• Boys and girls
• Different skin tones, clothing styles
• Rural and urban backgrounds
• One in a wheelchair, one holding a tablet, one with a robot

Center text: "AI works best when we all build it—together."

App Lab

Try Canva AI or Voiceflow and create:
• A poster that encourages girls in AI
• A simple voice bot that explains AI terms in your mother tongue
Present your creations during your school's AI Day!

Did You Know?

The world's first computer programmer was a woman—Ada Lovelace—in the 1800s!
She imagined that computers could do more than math—even music and art.
She dreamed it before it existed. Just like you can.

Master Insight

Technical Lens (Abeer)
The most valuable future skill will be understanding how to collaborate with intelligent systems.
Innovation Lens (Amaara)
Adaptability, creativity, and ethical judgment will differentiate human leaders from automated systems.

Summary

Here's what we learned:

- AI should be built by everyone—girls, boys, and all communities
- More diversity = better AI tools for all
- Girls face challenges—but they're rising as leaders
- Boys can support and uplift inclusion
- Inclusive AI starts in your school, team, and mindset

Remember: Your voice matters. Your code matters. Your vision matters.

No matter who you are, you belong in AI.

Chapter 12

Build Your Own AI Path

Study Plans, Courses, Mentors & Competitions

Want to learn AI seriously and turn it into a future career?
Great news—you can start right now, no matter your age or background!
This chapter is your AI learning roadmap. From free online courses to coding bootcamps, school clubs to global contests—we'll guide you step-by-step.
Let's build your custom journey into the world of Artificial Intelligence.

Step 1: Know Your Learning Level

Start by asking yourself:

Age/Grade	Focus Area
Grades 6–8	AI concepts, logic games, block coding
Grades 9–10	Python basics, datasets, beginner AI tools

Grades 11–12	AI models, real-world projects, ethics, career planning

You don't need to rush. Just be consistent and curious!

Step 2: Choose the Right Tools & Platforms

Here are beginner-friendly platforms to explore:

For Starters:
• Teachable Machine – No-code model training
• Scratch + ML – Block coding with machine learning
• Canva AI – Creative designs with AI

For Intermediate Learners:
• MIT App Inventor – Build your own Android apps
• Machine Learning for Kids – Train simple AI models with text, images
• Code.org AI Lab – Play-based AI experiments

For Advanced Teens:
• Google Colab – Write and run Python AI code
• Kaggle – AI competitions with real-world data
• Microsoft Learn AI Path – Structured modules for youth

Tip: Set a goal like "Complete 1 project per month" to stay on track.

Step 3: Practice with Mini Projects

Apply what you learn. Try:
• Mood-recognition using webcam
• Build a chatbot that answers fun questions
• Make a quiz app in your regional language
• Create an AI-generated art gallery
• Design a crop health predictor for farmers

Keep a portfolio—a simple Google Drive or blog that shows what you've built.

Step 4: Explore AI Courses – Free & Paid

Free Online Courses:

Platform	**Course**
CBSE + Intel	AI4Youth Modules
Google AI	AI for Anyone (India-specific)
IBM SkillsBuild	AI basics for students
Microsoft Learn	Intro to AI for Teens
Coursera (Audit mode)	AI for Everyone – Andrew Ng

Bonus: Many of these come with free certificates!

Paid (But Affordable) Courses:

Platform	Age	Cost
WhiteHat Jr	6–18	₹₹₹
Udemy	12+	₹₹ (often on sale)
Coding Ninjas	14+	₹₹₹
Vedantu AI Series	13–18	₹₹

Tip: Ask your school to sponsor a course for top AI learners.

Step 5: Find a Mentor or AI Guide

A mentor helps you stay motivated, solve problems, and dream bigger.

Where to Find One:
- School teachers

- Local coding club heads
- Online platforms like Codeavour, Github, TinkerHub
- College students studying AI
- Youth groups on platforms like Discord or Telegram

Join forums like Kaggle Community, Girls Who Code, or AI4Youth India to connect.

Step 6: Participate in AI Competitions

AI is more fun when you create and compete!

Indian & Global Challenges:

- ATL Marathon (CBSE) – For school AI projects
- Codeavour International AI Challenge
- Technovation Girls
- Smart India Hackathon (Junior Category)
- RoboCup Junior India
- Tinkerpreneur by AIM NITI Aayog

Prizes include laptops, scholarships, and mentoring by real scientists!

Try It Yourself!

Activity: Create Your AI Learning Plan

Draw a 6-month plan. Include:

- What tools to explore
- Which course to finish
- What project to complete
- Which competition to join
- Who could mentor you

Post it on your study wall or AI club board!

Think & Reflect

If you had access to all the AI tools and guidance, what kind of change would you want to bring to your school, town, or country? Think big. Now write a few steps to begin.

School Checklist – Start Your AI Journey Today

Form an AI Club
Host monthly learning sessions
Invite guest speakers from tech fields
Display student projects in exhibitions
Start a "Women in AI" poster series
Celebrate "AI Day" every year with demos and games
Ask your teacher to make it a part of the ICT/Computer period!

App Lab

Try Koo App AI Translator Tool – Used in India to convert posts across languages using AI.
Explore how language AI works—and think how you can apply it in school notes, quizzes, or even song lyrics!

Pro Tips from Young AI Achievers

"Don't wait to be perfect. Just start. My first AI project didn't even work, but my second one won an award."
— Mehak, Class 9, Delhi

"I used AI to make a voice assistant for my Dadi who speaks only Marathi."
— Atharv, Class 8, Pune

"I'm scared of math, but I love stories—so I use AI to write scripts for animation!"
— Fatima, Class 10, Lucknow

Everyone's path is different. The important thing is to start walking.

Infographic Suggestion

Title: "Your AI Learning Journey"

Draw a staircase or roadmap showing:
1. Start small (Scratch, Canva AI)
2. Learn tools (Teachable Machine, ML for Kids)
3. Build mini projects
4. Join a course
5. Find a mentor
6. Enter a competition
7. Dream big: Startup, Scientist, Storyteller

Use icons and checkboxes with progress levels.

Summary

Let's map your AI future:
- Start with easy tools
- Practice with mini projects
- Learn from free or guided courses
- Find mentors or communities
- Participate in AI challenges
- Showcase your journey!

There's no single way to learn AI. The best path is the one you create, step by step—with passion, patience, and purpose.

Chapter 13

India's AI Mission

Digital India, AI for Youth & Beyond

Artificial Intelligence is not just a global trend—it's a national mission for India.

With more than 1.4 billion people, 22+ official languages, and a fast-growing youth population, India needs AI that is inclusive, local, ethical, and powerful.

In this chapter, we explore how the Indian government, schools, and youth programs are building an AI-powered future—and how you can be part of it!

What Is India's AI Mission?

India's national vision is to make the country a global leader in AI that:

- Solves social problems
- Promotes economic growth

• Supports inclusive digital development
• Trains millions of youth in AI skills

This is being done through government strategies, education reforms, startups, and public-private partnerships.

NITI Aayog's National Strategy for AI

India's think tank, NITI Aayog, created a detailed plan titled:
"AI for All: #AIFORALL"

Key Focus Areas:
1. Healthcare – AI for disease diagnosis and affordable treatment
2. Agriculture – Precision farming and crop management
3. Education – AI-powered personalized learning
4. Smart Cities – Traffic, safety, and waste management using AI
5. Mobility & Transport – Self-driving, public systems, predictive traffic

India wants to become the "AI Garage for the World"—a place where affordable, ethical, and inclusive AI is built.

Digital India: AI in Action

The Digital India Mission has accelerated tech access across the country.

AI is being used in:
• Face authentication for Aadhaar services
• MyGov voice chatbots for public services
• Online language translation tools (e.g., Bhashini)
• Crop prediction and rainfall alerts for farmers
• AI-based drone surveys in Smart Cities

Example: The Ganga Water Monitoring AI helps track pollution levels using satellite and sensor data.

AI for Youth Program (AI4Youth)

Launched in collaboration with Intel, this national initiative empowers high school students to learn AI through real projects.

Highlights:
- For students of Grades 8–12
- Hands-on training in Python, Teachable Machine, Chatbots, Design Thinking
- Project showcase at school, district, and national levels
- Focus on ethics, problem-solving, and AI for social good

Thousands of CBSE students have built projects like:
- Disaster alert systems
- AI-based Braille converters
- Smart quiz bots for rural students

You can join this through your school's ATL or ICT department.

CBSE's AI Curriculum

Since 2019, CBSE has included AI as an elective subject for Grades 9–12.

Curriculum Covers:
- Basics of AI, ML, data, algorithms
- Tools like Scratch, Python, AI Project Cycle
- Real-life use cases
- Ethical guidelines and digital responsibility

Bonus: Students can present AI projects as part of their ICT grades or ATL innovation challenges.

AI in Indian Startups

India has a booming startup scene—with over 4,500 AI startups across sectors.

Notable examples:
• CropIn – AI for smart agriculture
• Qure.ai – AI for reading X-rays and brain scans
• Staqu – Police crime prediction using facial AI
• Niramai – Non-invasive cancer detection
• Embibe – AI-powered education and coaching

Many of these companies hire teens as interns or innovation ambassadors!

Try It Yourself!

Activity: Build an "AI for Bharat" Idea
Think of a local issue in your area: traffic, school dropouts, water waste, etc.

Now answer:
1. What is the problem?
2. How could AI help solve it?
3. Who would benefit?
4. How can you test it in your community?

Example: A WhatsApp AI bot that explains government schemes to farmers in Hindi.

Think & Reflect

India has over 200 languages and multiple cultures. Should AI tools always support regional languages?

Why is it important to build AI tools that work for everyone, not just English speakers or urban users?
Write your thoughts.

Key Government Programs Supporting AI

Program	**What It Does**
Atal Tinkering Labs (ATL)	Innovation labs in 10,000+ schools
Rural Digital Literacy Mission	Brings AI awareness to villages
Responsible AI Guidelines (MeitY)	Promotes fairness, privacy, ethics
AI in School Curriculum	Promotes future readiness
IndiaAI Portal	One-stop hub for AI policies, tools, and updates

Visit indiaai.gov.in for updates and contests!

Youth Stories That Inspire

Kriti, Class 10 – Haryana
Built an AI bot that helps students learn math in Haryanvi.

Arjun, Class 9 – Tamil Nadu
Designed a drone + AI system to detect garbage levels in his town.

Ritu, Class 12 – Jharkhand
Used AI to predict village dropout rates and presented her model to local authorities.
They started with school ideas. Now they are changemakers.

App Lab

Try the Bhashini AI Translator (India's language AI project). Type a sentence in English and translate it into 10+ Indian languages. Can you imagine building your own multilingual quiz app or health tips bot?

Career Corner: AI Roles Aligned with India's Needs

India's AI future needs professionals like:

- Agri-AI Technologist
- Health AI Analyst (rural outreach)
- Voice AI Developer (for Indian languages)
- EdTech Innovator
- Public Policy AI Advisor
- Social Media AI Strategist (for elections, awareness)

AI in India isn't just about tech—it's about impact, reach, and inclusion.

Infographic Suggestion

Title: "India's AI Revolution – For the People, By the People"
Include:

- NITI Aayog's 5 key sectors
- Logos of Digital India, CBSE AI, AI4Youth
- 3 student success stories (with small portraits)
- Timeline: 2019 – AI curriculum → 2020 – AI4Youth → 2023 – IndiaAI Summit

Use tricolor themes and icons like students, farmers, teachers, and coders.

Summary

Let's wrap up India's AI journey so far:

- **National strategy:** AI for All, not just a few

- **Education:** CBSE, ATL, AI4Youth programs
- Students are building real solutions
- Startups solving India-specific challenges
- Career paths for AI + impact-driven youth

India's AI mission is not about catching up with the world—it's about leading in a way that includes everyone.
The future of AI is Indian. And it includes you.

Chapter 14

Do's and Don'ts in an AI World

Be Smart, Be Safe, Be Kind

AI is amazing. But just like with the internet, we need to use it wisely. Think of AI like a bicycle. It can take you far—but only if you ride it safely and follow traffic rules. The same goes for AI. Whether you're using it or building it, you need to follow a code of responsibility.

In this chapter, we'll learn the best practices, common mistakes, and how to be a smart, safe, and kind digital citizen in the AI world.

The AI User's Code: Golden Do's

Here are the top things you should do when using or creating AI:

1. Do Understand the Basics

Know what AI is, how it works, and where it's used. This helps you use it better and not fall for myths.

2. Do Check the Source

Always ask:
• Who made this AI tool or app?
• Is it safe to use?
• Is it real or fake?
Download only from trusted sources.

3. Do Respect Privacy

Only share your:
• Name
• Photos
• Voice
• Location
on platforms that clearly tell you how your data is used.

Tip: Turn off microphone or camera access if not needed.

4. Do Think Before You Share
If an AI-generated message, video, or photo seems odd or too surprising—pause.

Ask:
Is it true?
Is it helpful?
Is it kind?
If not—don't share.

The AI User's Red Flags: Don'ts

Avoid these risky behaviors:

1. Don't Use AI to Cheat
Whether it's writing your homework or answering quizzes, using AI to cheat hurts your own learning.
Instead, use it to understand concepts, practice, or get hints.

2. Don't Pretend AI Is Human

Be clear when something is AI-made. Don't try to fool people by saying:

- "I wrote this poem" (when AI did)
- "This is a real photo" (when it's a deepfake)

Honesty matters.

3. Don't Use AI to Bully or Prank

Fake messages, images, or voice mimics can seriously hurt someone. That's not funny—it's dangerous. It could even lead to legal trouble.

Never use AI to:

- Mock someone
- Send anonymous threats
- Create fake videos or voices

4. Don't Overuse AI

If you let AI do everything—thinking, writing, answering—you stop growing.

Use it as a helper, not your brain's replacement.

Quick Comparison: Smart AI User vs. Risky AI User

Behavior	Smart AI User	Risky AI User
Uses AI for schoolwork	To practice and explore	To copy answers
Shares content	Only after verifying	Forwards anything
Makes content	With honesty	Passes AI work as own
Thinks about safety	Uses trusted tools	Gives data freely
Communicates	Kindly, ethically	Fakes voices or images

Try It Yourself!

Activity: Create an AI Safety Poster

Design a classroom poster titled:
"AI Is Powerful—Use It Wisely!"

Include:
• 3 Do's
• 3 Don'ts
• 1 tip for protecting privacy
• 1 example of good AI use

Add emojis, icons, or quotes like "Just because AI can do it, doesn't mean I should."

Think & Reflect

If a friend uses AI to cheat in an online test, what should you do? Would you ignore it? Report it? Talk to them? Why?
Write your response as a short journal entry titled: "Doing the Right Thing in the AI Age."

Laws & Rules You Should Know

India is working on laws to make AI safer.

Key Guidelines:
• Consent is important—apps must tell you what they collect
• Age-appropriate tools—Some AI platforms are only for 13+
• Harmful use = Punishment—Fake voice videos can lead to police action
• School policies—Cheating with AI may result in lower grades

Always read privacy policies and terms of use (even if boring!).

Real-Life Mistakes to Learn From

Deepfake Trouble
A student used an AI tool to fake a teacher's voice and posted it online. It went viral.
Result? Suspension, apology letter, and digital training course.

AI Image Scam
Someone shared AI-generated flood images and claimed they were real. People panicked. The source was later exposed—and blocked.
Lesson: Use AI with truth and care.

Your AI Responsibility Pledge

Make your own AI Pledge:
"I promise to use AI tools safely, fairly, and honestly.
I will never use them to harm, trick, or cheat.
I will protect my data and respect others online."
Sign it. Share it. Live it.

App Lab

Try Be Internet Awesome (by Google)

It teaches:
- Online safety
- Spotting scams
- Sharing responsibly
- AI-generated content awareness

Play games like "Reality River" to practice safe choices.

Tips from Student Leaders

"I use AI for fun but never to lie. Honesty is cooler than cheating."
— Raghav, Class 8

"I added a note saying 'AI helped me write this' in my project."
— **Mehak, Class 9**

"When my friend made an AI joke video of our teacher, I told him to delete it. Not everything is funny."
— **Zoya, Class 10**

Infographic Suggestion

Title: "AI Etiquette – Be Smart, Be Safe, Be Kind"

Divide into 3 sections with icons:

1. Be Smart – Learn, question, grow
2. Be Safe – Check sources, protect data
3. Be Kind – Respect, don't misuse AI

Add reminders like:

- "Think before you share"
- "Ask before uploading someone's photo"
- "Say it's AI-made if it is"

Summary

Let's lock in the basics of smart AI behavior:

- Do use AI to learn and grow
- Don't cheat, trick, or harm with AI
- Do check facts before forwarding or posting
- Don't overshare personal data
- Do be honest about what AI helped you with
- Don't let AI replace your thinking or values

In this fast-paced digital world, your behavior matters more than the bot's.

So be the kind, curious, and careful AI user the world needs.

Chapter 15

Final Quiz & Challenge Section

Can You Spot the AI?

Congratulations!
You've learned what AI is, how it works, where it's used, how to build with it, and how to use it safely and ethically. But are you ready to test your AI knowledge and detective skills?

This final chapter is your challenge zone—a mix of quizzes, games, reflection tasks, and real-life spotting exercises to see how much you've understood.
Let's see if you can truly think like an AI explorer!

Section 1: The Big AI Quiz

Choose the correct answer (MCQs):

1. What is Artificial Intelligence?
a) Robots only
b) Machine that feels emotions

c) Tech that mimics human thinking
d) A new toy
Answer: c

2. Which tool helps you train AI with no code?
a) Microsoft Paint
b) Teachable Machine
c) PowerPoint
d) WhatsApp

Answer: b

3. What is a common danger of AI misuse?
a) Speeding up games
b) Automatic spelling correction
c) Deepfakes and fake content
d) Better search results

Answer: c

4. AI learns using...
a) Emotions
b) Magic
c) Data and patterns
d) Copy-paste

Answer: c

5. Who was the world's first computer programmer?
a) Steve Jobs
b) Sundar Pichai
c) Ada Lovelace
d) Rani Lakshmibai

Answer: c

Section 2: Spot the AI

Read each situation. Decide: Is it AI or Not AI?

1. Your phone unlocks by scanning your face.
→ **AI**

2. A calculator solves 453 × 62.
→ **Not AI (it doesn't learn)**

3. YouTube recommends videos you like.
→ **AI**

4. A light switch turns on manually.
→ **Not AI**

5. Google Translate changes "Namaste" into "Hello."
→ **AI**

Section 3: Real vs AI-Made

Can you tell which of the following were created by humans and which by AI?

Image of a man with six fingers on one hand, glowing eyes, and a melted background.
→ **Likely AI-generated (watch for visual glitches)**

Poem about a robot that ends with "I am not real, but I dream in code."
→ **Could be AI-written (check for pattern and tone)**

Song with perfect beat matching, but no emotional ups and downs.
→ **Likely AI-generated music**

Tip: AI often gets structure right but feeling wrong.

Section 4: Build-Your-Own Mini AI Challenge

Your Task:

Create a mini project idea based on the following clues:
- **Problem:** Students forget homework deadlines
- **Tool:** Chatbot or voice assistant
- **Data:** Calendar + reminder inputs
- **Feature:** Sends alerts based on subject

Now sketch or describe your AI's name, features, and how students will use it. Share with a friend or teacher!

Section 5: Critical Thinking

Question 1:
Should there always be a human behind every AI decision (like hiring, exams, arrests)? Why or why not?

Write 4–5 sentences.
Include points about fairness, accountability, and feelings.

Question 2:
A classmate creates an AI bot that spreads funny, but fake, school gossip. What would you do?

Write a short paragraph with your response and explain how it affects safety and truth.

Section 6: Your AI Certificate Goals

You've already completed this book! Now make a real plan:
I want to:

- Join my school's AI club
- Take a beginner coding course
- Build one AI project in 3 months
- Join an AI competition this year
- Share an AI idea at school assembly

Share your goal with a mentor or classmate to stay accountable!

Bonus Activity: "AI Detective Day" at School

Host a class challenge where everyone:

- Brings 1 example of AI they found at home
- Presents 1 fun AI tool or app
- Votes on "Best AI For Good" project idea
- Decorates a wall board: "How AI Helps Our Life"

Encourage badges like:

- "Most Creative AI Idea"
- "Kindest AI Project"
- "Best Teamwork in AI"

App Lab

Try the "This Person Does Not Exist" site. It shows faces created by AI that look real—but aren't!

Can you:

- Spot signs of AI glitches (like extra teeth, uneven ears)?
- Think of how such tools could be misused or used ethically?

Infographic Suggestion

Title: "AI Challenge Tracker – What Have I Learned?"
Create a grid of:

- AI Tools I Used

- Projects I Built
- Quizzes I Took
- People I Taught About AI
- Skills I Gained

Decorate it as a personal tracker to reflect on your growth.

Master Insight

Technical Lens (Abeer)
Mastery of AI requires continuous learning. Tools evolve — foundational understanding remains.
Innovation Lens (Amaara)
Leadership in the AI age means shaping technology for societal benefit, not just personal advantage.

Summary

Let's review your AI journey:
- You learned the 5Ws of AI
- Explored how AI works with data and learning
- Discovered its use in real life and big industries
- Built beginner projects
- Discussed ethics, safety, and inclusion
- Met role models, future jobs, and India's AI vision
- Took the final quiz like a true AI explorer!

Give yourself a round of applause—you're no longer just an AI user. You're now an AI citizen, builder, and thinker

Parting Thought

"Don't just use AI. Shape it.
Don't just follow AI. Lead it.
The future needs your heart, your mind, and your ideas."
Go ahead—create, question, explore, and dream with AI.
Because the world is waiting for your genius.

Glossary Of Key Ai Terms

Term	Simple Definition
AI (Artificial Intelligence)	Technology that helps machines think and act like humans.
Algorithm	A set of rules or steps a computer follows to solve problems.
Data	Information (numbers, images, words) that AI uses to learn.
Machine Learning (ML)	A way for machines to learn from data and improve over time.
Neural Network	A system inspired by the human brain that helps computers recognize patterns.
Deep Learning	A type of machine learning that uses complex neural networks to solve harder problems.
Chatbot	A computer program that talks with humans, usually online.
Facial Recognition	A tool that helps AI recognize and identify faces.
Natural Language Processing (NLP)	Technology that helps machines understand human language.
Supervised Learning	When AI learns from labeled examples (e.g., photos tagged "cat").
Unsupervised Learning	When AI looks at data without labels and finds patterns.

Bias	When AI gives unfair results because of poor or limited training data.
Teachable Machine	A beginner-friendly AI tool from Google to train a model without coding.
DALL•E	An AI tool that creates images from text descriptions.
Deepfake	Fake videos or photos created using AI that look very real.
Digital Responsibility	Using technology safely, kindly, and wisely.
AI for Good	Projects where AI helps people, the environment, or society.
Data Privacy	Protecting your personal information online.
India Stack	A set of digital tools by the Indian government that support digital services like Aadhaar and UPI.
Ethical AI	AI that is fair, transparent, and used for good purposes.
Prompt	A message or instruction given to an AI to get a response.